The Art of the Birdhouse

Portraits of Artists and their Creations

The Art of the Birdhouse:
Portraits of Artists and their Creations

Copyright © 2006 by Project Return.
All rights reserved. Printed in China.
No part of this book may be used or reproduced in
any manner whatsoever, without written permission,
except in the context of reviews.

For additional information contact:
Project Return, 124 Compo Road North
Westport, Connecticut 06880

ISBN: 0-9776000-0-9
SAN: 257-7275
Library of Congress Control Number: 2005910165

Cover photos, clockwise from upper left:
Robert Goodenow; photo by Mike Tewey
Humpty Dumpty Sat on a Nest by Suzanne Ebeling-Urban; photo by Alison Wachstein
Joanne Woodward & Paul Newman; photo by Miggs Burroughs
English Style Stone Cottage by Kassie Foss; photo by Mike Tewey

About Project Return

Birdhouses, safe and nurturing environments, symbolize the work of Project Return, a group home for adolescent girls in crisis in Westport, Connecticut. Project Return enables young teens to rebuild their lives through individualized treatment, emphasizing the development of self-awareness, well-being and purpose. Director Susie Basler has guided Project Return since its beginning 20 years ago and has infused the endeavor with caring and enthusiasm.

The Art of the Birdhouse is a celebration of ten years of birdhouse auctions, held to raise funds to support Project Return. What started in 1996 with just a handful of local artists has evolved into an event with close to 200 artists joining in a show of heartfelt communal support. Over 850 artists have taken part in the auction in the last ten years. Showcased each year are the artists' varied talents with birdhouses that are fanciful, thematic, outrageous, simple or elaborate, big and small. This book reunites many of these artists with their special art.

Grateful thanks are extended to all the artists who participate in this project each year and to the photographers who have given their time and talent to make this book possible. Proceeds from the sale of *The Art of the Birdhouse* will provide additional funding for Project Return, benefiting the girls this organization was established to serve.

Book Credits

Designer:
Miggs Burroughs

Production:
Sydney Watras

Writers:
Thomas Asher, Michael Fanning, Totney Benson

Editors:
Nina Bentley, Kim Cooper, Sydney Watras

Committee:
**Susie Basler, Nina Bentley, Totney Benson,
Miggs Burroughs, Kim Cooper, Lorin Klaris,
Jeannette Tewey, Mick Tewey, Sydney Watras**

Totney Benson

Totney, who hatched the idea for the Birdhouse Auction, continues her involvement and is an expert at processing hundreds of birdhouses each year at her home, 'birdhouse central.' She orchestrated the brief reuniting of the artists with their birdhouses for the photographs in this book.

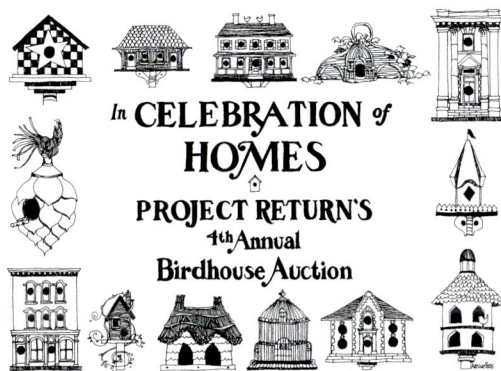

Kassie Foss

Kassie became involved with the birdhouse auction at its inception and designed the first logo in her signature pen-and-ink style. Each year, through the tenth anniversary, she has created logos depicting imaginative birdhouses, often using the building that houses Project Return as her inspiration. Examples of her black and white art appear above and throughout the opening pages of this book.

We extend our sincere gratitude to the following
Project Return supporters who have generously
contributed, in equal share, to the production costs for
The Art of the Birdhouse. As a result, all proceeds
from the sale of this book will go directly to support
Project Return's ongoing good works.

Gault, Inc.
Resnick Investment Advisors, LLC
Neal & Carolyn Barton
Andrew Bentley & Fiona Garland
Patricia Burrows & Milt Wolfson
Ellen & Thomas Granger
David Himmelreich
Ann Sheffer & Bill Scheffler
Sam Small
Jeannette & Mike Tewey

Table of Contents

Nina & Richard Bentley 10	Marta Flavin 68
Elise Black 12	Richard Flowers .70
Arthur Burke 14	Patricia Scanlan .72
Ann Chernow 16	Kassie & Larry Foss 74
Judy Henderson & Hans Wilhelm 18	Meredith Donaher 76
Miggs Burroughs .20	Donald & Kelly Quatrella 78
Joanne Woodward & Paul Newman 22	Jane Horton 80
Lewis & Marilyn Cohen 24	John BonSignore 82
Constance Keirmaier 26	Dawn Rogers 84
Audrey & Drew Klotz 28	Naiad & Walter Einsel 86
Suzanne Henrick 30	Robert Goodenow 88
Rick Benson 32	Eve Stockton 90
Howard & Andrew Munce 34	Tori Letzler 92
Dick & Marilee Reilly 36	Susan Malloy 94
Katherine Ross 38	Susan Lloyd 96
Helene Dworski .40	Enid Munroe 98
Barbara (Bobbie) Herman 42	Winston Potter .100
Carol Brezovec & Cathy Osterhout 44	Mike Tewey 102
Martha Bloom 46	Van Ruttley 104
Amy Riggio 48	Ellen Schiffman 106
Karen Silver Bloom 50	Kathi Sherman .108
Manny Pattavina 52	Dick Stein 110
Sallie Hackett Brown 54	Robert Schwarz 112
Maryann Charmoz 56	Ann Weiner 114
John Waski 58	Carol Young 116
Steve Delay 60	More Birdhouses 118
Lucy Sallick 62	Photographers .122
Lucy Krupenye .64	Birdhouse Artists & Other Contributors . .123
Leslie Giuliani 66	Birdhouse Owners 127

Nina, an assemblage artist of international reputation, normally does work which represents a form of social commentary, at times humorous, but always insightful. Her birdhouses, including "Welcome to Wallport", "Louis Tweeton", and "Building Plans Approved: The Planning and Dozing Committee," poke fun at life in post-modern suburbia. For me," she says, "making them is, quite simply, a lark!"

Richard, once a businessman, now an educator, claims modesty requires he admit that he only creates when inspired by his Muse. The result is always surprising, especially for him. "My art," he says, "may be seen as a kind of accident and, at the outset of any new endeavor, as an accident waiting to happen."

Nina & Richard Bentley

Nina, Assemblage Artist
Richard, Businessman and Educator

Stool Pigeon, Birdie Hole (left page)
Location, Location, Location (above, left)
Louis Tweeton (above, right)
Welcome to Wallport (right)
Building Plans Approved: The Planning & Dozing Committee (left)

Photos by Miggs Burroughs

Elise Black
Artist

"I enjoy using found elements and objects that have unique sculptural form." In the birdhouse artwork, "all of these elements come together to create a form that is abstracted yet implies the 'idea' of a birdhouse." Elise, a multi-media artist and designer specializing in site-specific projects and works of art, says, "Project Return is an organization whose mission holds a special place in my heart. To me, it's the embodiment of female solidarity. I can't think of a better source of inspiration for creating a birdhouse." Elise's large, public sculptures, as well as her smaller works, are nationally exhibited and collected.

Elements

Photos by Lorin Klaris

Discarded light fixtures, trashed mail boxes, forgotten doll houses as objets d'art? Yes, if you take pride and satisfaction in making one man's trash into another's artistic treasure. Arthur, always paying meticulous attention to detail, has made 123 box assemblages from these finds. His discerning eye led him to hire a young Andy Warhol, in his first career as a display designer. Arthur then went on to have a highly successful career as an interior designer-artist. A gentleman who embodies an old world work ethic, he says, "I always gave my clients a little more than they bargained for," and that's just what he does for Project Return.

Arthur Burke
Interior Designer, Artist

Faberge Aviary (left & above)
Singer's Aviary (above, right)
Cornell House for Birds (right)

Photos by Lorin Klaris

Only the most elegant of hens can choose such a classy home as this Louis Vuitton bag, created by Ann Chernow, Westport based, renowned artist. Ann's work in mixed media, drawing and printmaking has been exhibited internationally and can be seen in the collections of the Metropolitan Museum of Art, Yale University and The Brooklyn Museum. Ann, owner of an exceptional collection of contemporary art, has a close connection with artists and recently completed the biography, begun by her late husband Bert, of Christo and his wife Jean Claude.

Designer Hen

Photos by Robin Fellows

Ann Chernow
Artist

Freedom Bird (above)

Matilda

Jack's Birdhouse (below)

Papagena

Judy Henderson & Hans Wilhelm

Judy, Ceramic Artist; Hans, Author, Illustrator

"As a ceramic artist I have always made vessels and other functional pieces to be used inside one's domain. The home, in a way, is a vessel and so is the heart. So, my birdhouses are vessels of love for the benefit of Project Return." Judy's ceramics, popular and treasured, are sold in many upscale stores, such as Henri Bendel in New York.

Hans, author and illustrator of the well-known book, *I'll Always Love You*, has more than 180 titles for children and adults to his credit, with more than 35,000,000 copies in print. His books have been translated into more than 200 languages and have won numerous international awards and prizes. Many of his stories have become successful animated television series.

Photos by Miggs Burroughs

Miggs Burroughs

Graphic Designer

"I realize now that all my birdhouses seem to provide a way of peering inside, architecturally and/or emotionally. They invite the viewer, myself included, to take a very personal house tour," says Miggs, reflecting on his long, ten year history of donated creations.

Miggs is an accomplished artist and graphic designer, with credits ranging from a commemorative U.S. postage stamp, hundreds of corporate logos and a presidential Easter egg to a TIME magazine cover now housed in the Smithsonian.

Unopened Rose (left page)
Changes (top)
The Gift (middle)
Tender Treasures (bottom)

Photos by
Pam Barkentin-Blackburn

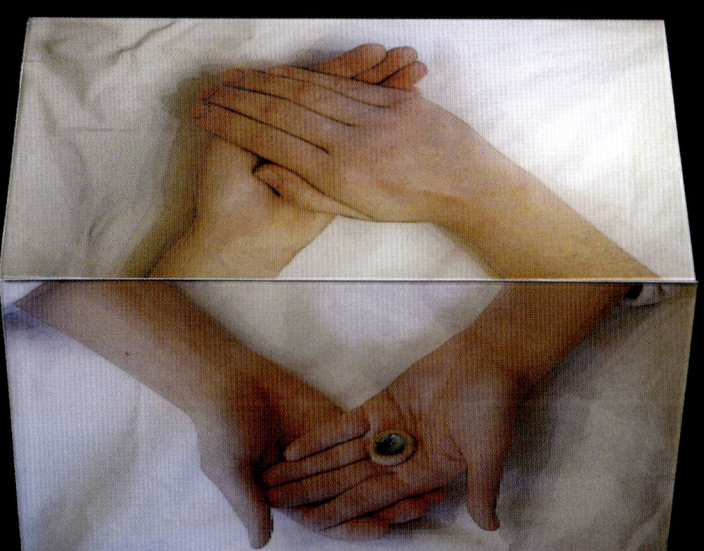

Joanne Woodward & Paul Newman

Actors, Philanthropists

International stars Joanne Woodward and Paul Newman have always supported local causes and been very generous with their time and money. Paul's charitable organization, Newman's Own, has sponsored the Birdhouse Auction every year since its inception. For their birdhouses, they have collaborated with their daughter Lissy, who is an artist in her own right. Joanne and Paul's art-adorned homes, covered with their drawings and autographs, were embellished by their daughter with charming and engaging results.

A Home is for Family

A Home for All

Photos by Miggs Burroughs

Lewis & Marilyn Cohen
Lewis: Film Maker, Artist; Marilyn: Designer, Artist

De Oily Boid (left)
Bird Watcher (above & right)
Art is for the Birds (middle right)
The White-Crested,
Migratory, Sun-Seeking Snowbird (far right)

Photos by Patrick Vingo

The genius of the Cohens' art springs from their years spent working in highly successful careers. Lewis was the creative head and owner of a New York City film production company. He currently teaches at the New York School of Visual Arts. Marilyn was an illustrator and designer of fabrics, wallpaper, handbags, toys and games. She now gathers oral histories and old family photos to save the personal stories of American history in creative, painting-like collages, rich in detail and texture. Lewis' birdhouses are often delightful visual puns made from found objects, paint and printed material. He appreciates the great value in oddities and allows us to see "the same old things" in new ways, with whimsy and humor.

Constance Kiermier's work often incorporates found objects and natural materials. Here, her use of natural pine planking, knotholes and all, recalls the true homes our feathered friends enjoy in the wild. Constance is an accomplished printmaker, painter, teacher and mentor who has been widely exhibited. Her talent has been recognized by Weir Farm as its Visiting Artist.

Fly Away Home (left)
Forest Birdhouse (right)

Photos by
Andrea Maritzer Fine

Constance Keirmaier
Artist

Award-winning artists Drew and Audrey Klotz are a great team, in life and art. Luckily for Project Return, they often work together using their talents to create lively birdhouses that combine motion, activity and humor, with moving parts and lights, sure to entertain, amuse and delight. Drew's wind-activated and other kinetic sculptures are installed in such places as Stepping Stones Museum in Norwalk, and at the Long Island Children's Museum. Audrey's mural work is on the walls of many Connecticut stores, her trompe d'oeil is in homes throughout Fairfield County and her fine art was recently chosen for the Silvermine's Biennial Show.

Drew & Audrey Klotz

Drew, Kinetic Sculptor;
Audrey, Muralist, Trompe d'Oeil Painter

Fried Chicken (above & left)
Moulin Rouge (right)

Photos by Kim Cooper

Suzanne Henrick

Nutritionist

Suzanne often works with the staff and residents of Project Return in her role as a nutritionist. She uses her creative side to support Project Return by making birdhouses for the auction. In this piece, the four sides of the candle create a connected scene of an impending storm. The storm represents the emotional turmoil in the girls' lives which brings them to Project Return. The bird in the corner represents freedom from the storm as it flies away to shelter. The concept of a candleholder symbolizes hope from a light within.

*Spring Rain Storm –
Seeking Shelter*

Photos by David Kalman

Bye Bye Birdie

Rick Benson
Real Estate Developer

A Victorian Home (top)
Waldheim Camp (middle)
Saugatuck Harbor Yacht Club (bottom)

Photos by Kim Cooper

Rick's amazingly detailed miniature reproductions of landmark buildings in Fairfield County reflect the quality of work and attention to detail that are found in his building of elaborate, custom-designed homes. For his replicas, he prepares scale drawings, architectural specs, elevations, photographs each façade and then hand-shapes hundreds of pieces of wood. Small wonder his creations are collectors' items, consistently bringing the highest bids at the annual Birdhouse Auction.

Howard & Andrew Munce

Howard: Artist, Advertising Executive
Andrew: Sculptor, Woodworker

The Bird-Brain House (right)
The Stool Pigeon House (below)

Photos by Miggs Burroughs

Howard is multi-talented: an illustrator, cartoonist, painter, humorist, sculptor, writer and former art director. He is 90 years old and is still the 'go-to-guy' for any kind of art. Howard has curated exhibits, designed books and received numerous awards. Often found doing good works around town, he contributes his talents generously, such as creating birdhouses for Project Return for all ten years. His talents are legendary; he is Professor Emeritus at Paier College of Art, Honorary President of the Society of Illustrators and an original member of the Famous Artists School.

Howard's son, Andrew, is a sculptor, wood-turner, carpenter and artist, whose work can be seen on the grounds of Housatonic Community College. He is currently the technical director of "Art in Public Places" in Stamford, Connecticut.

The Crofter's Cottage
Bound for Glory (railroad car)
Bronson Windmill

Photos by Ron Henkih

Dick & Marilee Reilly

Dick, Builder; Marilee, Artist

Dick is an accomplished builder and architectural preservationist with award-winning renovations of historic homes to his credit. His models can be seen at the Mill Hill Historical Society and the Norwalk Museum. Dick collaborates on true-to-life Birdhouse Auction creations with his wife Marilee. Each birdhouse is made by Dick from recycled materials, with careful attention to detail, and is adorned by Marilee's artistic touches. Dedicated supporters of Project Return, they have contributed to the birdhouse auction each of its ten years. To celebrate the tenth year, and in commemoration of 9/11, he created an exact replica of a New York City firehouse call box. Bought by a supporter, it is now displayed in the lobby of a building in the same precinct as the original on which it is based.

Katherine Ross

Artist

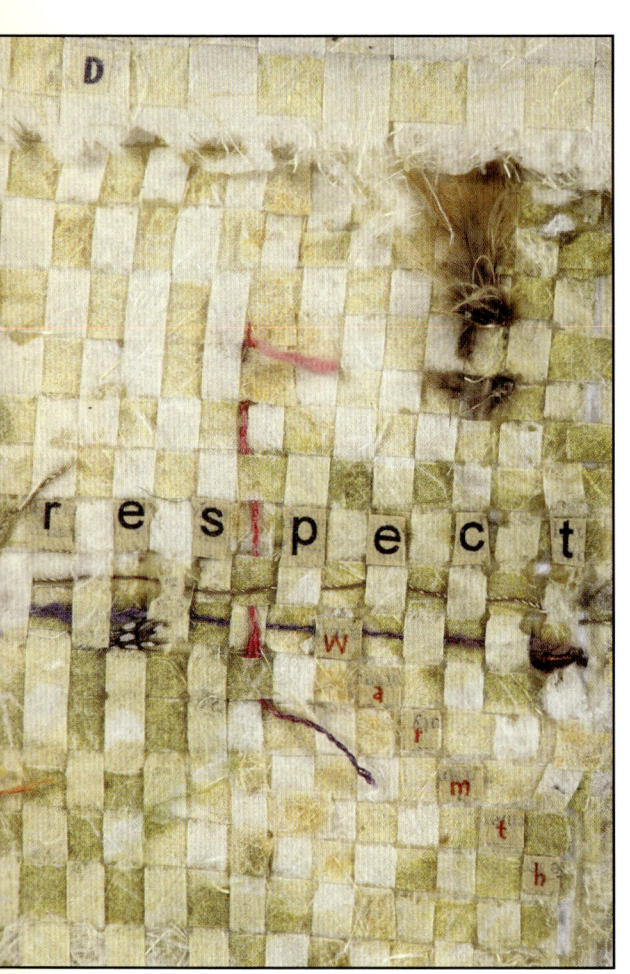

Painter and watercolorist, Katherine creates houses which "are shelters for fragile beings, for hearts that need protection, and homes that offer freedom from lives constrained." Her designs convey the essence of what Project Return is all about. Katherine's concern for others extends to her teaching art to young children and to her support and promotion of art in the public schools. She has involved her students in interactive mural art in public spaces.

Woven (left)

Nina's Wings

Photos by
Mary Ellen Hendricks

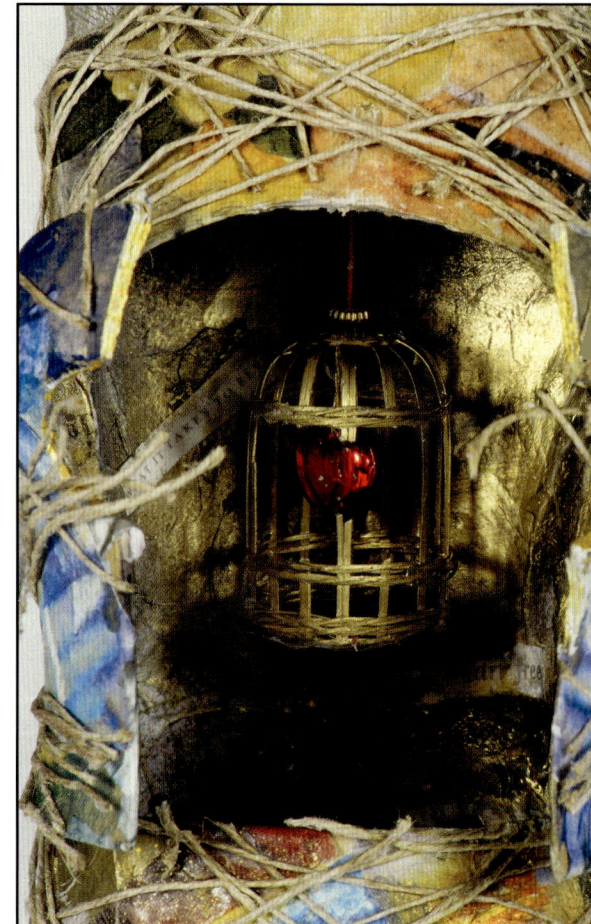

Helene Dworski
Designer

Covering a wooden birdhouse with over 70,000 tiny beads, each one hand-placed in a beeswax resin using a toothpick, was a process Helene took 90 hours to complete. In this highly unusual birdhouse, the design she created on the wood shows through the resin, producing subtle shadings, almost like a tapestry. This seems very natural for a former designer and textile specialist for Lillian August. Her last two birdhouses were miniature upholstered furniture. Helene has her own beaded jewelry and painted clothing company. Her jewel-like creations have become some of the most sought after artwork at the Birdhouse Auction.

Bead Bird, Wing Chair

Photos by Debra K. Browne

Barbara (Bobbie) Herman
Appraiser, Actress

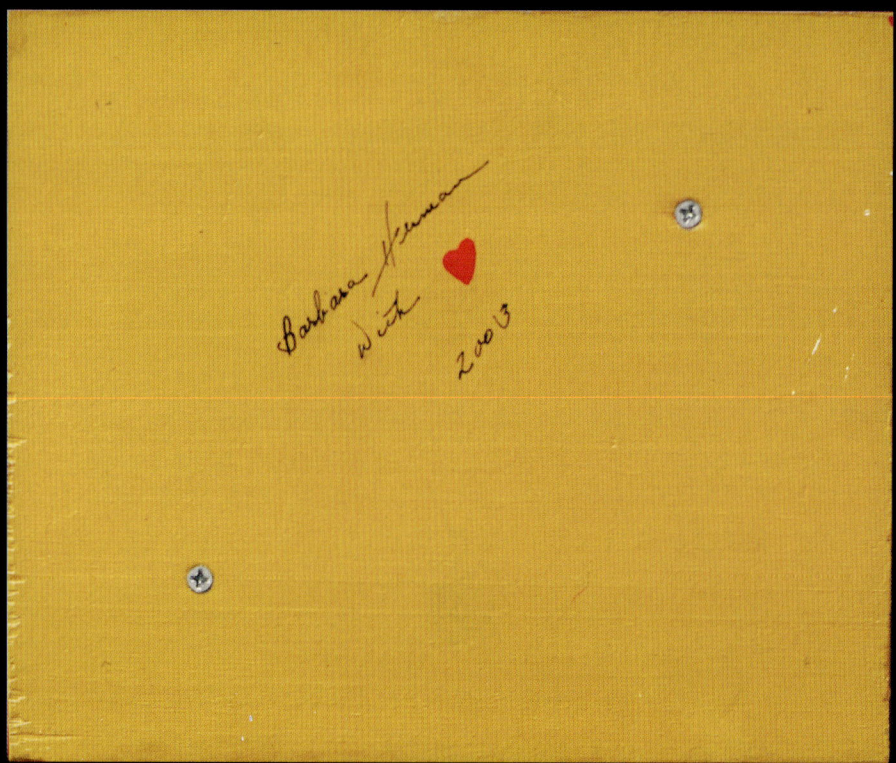

Bobbie is one of Project Return's original birdhouse creators and has generously taken the time to craft a birdhouse each year since the auction's inception. A real estate appraiser by profession, Bobbie knows a good house when she makes one, and is excited by American Folk Art and the Primitive style. Sporting a patriotic theme here, Bobbie, with the attack of September 11 painfully fresh in her mind, created a birdhouse which reaffirmed her love of her country. Bobbie has won several "best in show" awards for her needlework and has displayed her artwork throughout Fairfield County. She is also a talented actress and appeared last year in "Pippin" in New Haven.

Stars & Stripes

Photos by Peter Friedman

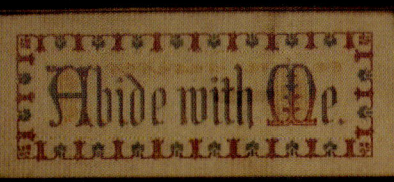

Carol Brezovec & Cathy Osterhout
Crafters

Partners in business and partners in support of Project Return, Carol and Cathy love crafts and, for many years, worked together in their business, C & C Designs, for which they created and sold wonderful items for the home. They continue to work together to create birdhouses for the auction, as they have done for all ten years.

Birdhouse Topiary, Funky Feathers & Fancy Feathers

Photos by John Hill

Martha continually scavenges material for her work and particularly appreciates the connections she creates when working with "collections of age." With an old cobbler's shoe, found deep in the woods of Vermont, she found "a nesting shape, female in form, suggestive of fertility and flight." Artist, photographer, performance artist and art teacher, Martha explains, "My artistic philosophy is to explore the physical boundaries between media and the conceptual boundaries between form, content, intent-accident and reality-dream."

Untitled

Photos by
Pam Einarsen

Martha Bloom
Artist, Teacher

Most of Amy's birdhouses are "time" themed. Her fixation with timepieces stems either from the fact that her husband Tony is a watchmaker, or the fact that Amy tackles so many jobs that her days need 36 hours. Amy's contribution extends beyond her birdhouse– she is a member of the Auction Committee and has been the co-chairman of the Evening Stroll Guided Tours of Birdhouses in downtown Westport for three years.

Time Flies I
Time Flies II
Photos by David Emberling

Amy Riggio
Crafter

Karen has found a medium which combines her two loves, collecting antiques and illustrating. She scours flea markets, antiques shows and tag sales for unusual toys, trims and treasures and incorporates her finds into one-of-a-kind collectibles. Her shadow boxes have brought her national recognition and appear in magazines coast to coast. For the Birdhouse Auction, her work reflects the spirit and goals of Project Return in such works as "Home Sweet Home" and "Happily Ever After."

Temptation (far left)
And They Lived Happily Ever After
Childlife (above & left)

Photos by David Kalman

Karen Silver Bloom

Artist

Manny Pattavina

Educator, Woodworker

For the past four years, Manny has contributed birdhouses that answer to a "higher authority." The churches throughout New England inspired his first birdhouse, "The Sanctuary." Manny says, "Since building my first birdhouse, it has inspired a new hobby that I am passionate about. I have built over one hundred houses so far, and no two are alike." After teaching woodworking for 35 years, Manny retired but still substitutes and is a teacher at the Woodworking Club of Norwalk.

The Sanctuary

Photos by Mike Tewey

Sallie Hackett Brown
Artist, Sculptor

This creative artist and former model was the inspiration for the song, "Mustang Sally," by Wilson Pickett. Sallie continues evolving her artistic persona by creating sculptures using wooden objects in new and unique ways. "The idea for my sculptures is often inspired by just one single element," she says. "I see an object and envision a whole new use for it, a way to bring out a design quality that perhaps was never intended to be." Sallie has exhibited widely in the Northeast and has won numerous awards.

Das Blau Bird Bauhaus

Photos by Bruce Ando

Maryann Charmoz
Artist

As Maryann was traveling to her home in the Berkshires one weekend, she spotted a family of odd-looking birds crossing the road in front of her—the shape and color of autumn gourds, dressed in raffia for warmth. She was inspired. She raced home and created these birdhouses. Maryanne is a talented painter who specializes in murals and also creates painted furniture and faux finishes in private homes and restaurants.

The Gourdy Bird Family

Photos by Larry Merz

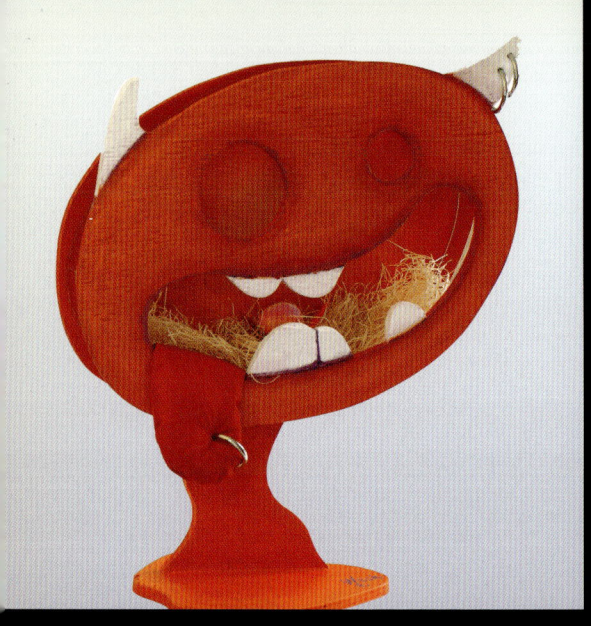

Cat House (above)
Scream

Photos by Hans Wilhelm

Zany, wacky, irreverent … vivid colors… John is the owner of John Waski Design, LLC, a Westport-based strategic brand identity and packaging design firm. He says "My approach to art is an emotional reaction to life's challenges and accomplishments."

John Waski

Artist

Steve Delay
Businessman

A retired printing executive, Steve has turned his life-long hobby of woodworking into a passion, producing pieces ranging from furniture to sculpture. His handsome birdhouses are elegant and sophisticated, appearing to be simple in design. They combine incredible workmanship, a bit of gold leaf and beautiful woods, including tiger maple, birds-eye maple, yellow heartwood, Indonesian rosewood and mahogany.

Birds Eye Birdhouse

Photos by Bruce Plotkin

Lucy Sallick
Painter, Printmaker

Charming the Birds (left)
Secret Designs (center)
Our House (right)

Photos by Roger Spencer Jones

Lucy, a painter and printmaker, has often made birdhouse art that reflects Project Return, "this most special house and home." She has been a visiting artist at the Weir Farm National Park Site in Wilton, and her work is in numerous public collections, including the University of Michigan Museum of Art, the Bruce Museum in Greenwich, Bowdoin College Museum of Art in Maine, and in many corporate and municipal collections.

Lucy's work illustrates how far the art of the birdhouse has come! "I created this birdhouse to represent a peaceful, loving, 'Zen' shelter for any 'bird' in need of one," she says. Lucy, who works primarily in stone, wood, metal and bone, has the ability to make combinations of these materials soothing and peaceful. She has won Awards of Excellence for Sculpture from the Montserat Gallery in New York City and the Stamford Museum in Connecticut.

Zen Shelter II

Photos by Martha Bloom

Leslie Giuliani
Artist, Teacher

Leslie is best known for her encaustic work in which she constructs paintings from layers of melted wax. She employed this technique to create her birdhouse, using a gourd for the base surface. Leslie's recent solo show at the Silvermine Guild in New Canaan, Connecticut, was enthusiastically received and set a record for gallery sales.

Bird Sanctuary

Photos by Miggs Burroughs

67

Marta Flavin

Artist, Realtor

Marta creates beautiful birdhouses using her fabulous painting skills and a touch of whimsy. She is a sought-after muralist and trompe d'oeil artist. A successful real estate agent and an avid rower, Marta draws her artistic strength from the beauty and serenity of nature. Her work has been featured in a Better Homes and Gardens' Special Interest Publication, "Kids Rooms."

Classic Home (left)
Compo Beach (this page)

Photos by Carol Verneuil

Richard Flowers

Sculptor

A retired chemist, Richard creates designs for his company, R. F. Steelworks. His metal structures grace gardens all over New England. Striking and sophisticated, his steel sculptures are simple in design and concept, yet truly art for the garden. The rich patina of the steel perfectly complements the sleek lines of his structures.

Rustic Retreat

Photos by Morgaine Pauker

Patricia Scanlan
Interior Designer

Tweet Tweet Bling Bling (left)
Compo Pavilion (above, middle)
Luminest (above, right)
The Iris Cottage (right page)

Photos by Mike Tewey

Patricia Scanlan has contributed generously to Project Return as a volunteer, board member and, of course, as an artist, creating a birdhouse each year of the auction. The magnificent look of the Birdhouse Auction over the years is due to Patricia's extraordinary expertise and inspiration in displaying the birdhouses and decorating, while, at the same time, arranging for the food and music! Professionally, she loves to design kitchens and libraries, with the objective of creating light and natural rooms, in a variety of styles.

Kassie & Larry Foss

Kassie, Watercolor Artist
Larry, Businessman, Woodworker

The birdhouses that Kassie and her husband Larry have created (he builds and she paints) reflect where they have lived: an English Cottage from their time in England, and Westport's landmarks such as the old library, the old town hall, and the Minuteman Yacht Club from their time in Connecticut. Kassie's well-known watercolors and pen-and-ink drawings can be found in private collections, books and the greeting cards from Onion Hill Designs of which she is co-owner. The first ten birdhouse auction invitations and logos displayed Kassie's illustrations of birdhouses or the Project Return house.

Cape Cod Contentment (left)
Old Town Hall (top right)
English Style Stone Cottage (bottom right)

Photos by Mike Tewey

Meredith is a high school student who has been making birdhouses for the auction for several years. Her family is a big supporter of Project Return and she has followed their example by giving of her time and talent. When not in school, she loves horseback riding and swimming.

Seaside Cottage

Photos by Debra Somerville

Meredith Donaher
High School Student

Donald & Kelly Quatrella

Don, Businessman; Kelly, Sales Manager

While remodeling his kitchen, Don salvaged several old seasoned pine boards that otherwise might have ended up in the dumpster. Salvaging the old planking and turning it into a functional birdhouse reminded him of Project Return's mission of helping teenage girls change their lives in a useful and positive way. Don often creates birdhouses that are replicas of well-known buildings or have a rustic feel. His wife, Kelly, a sales manager, constructed a garden shed birdhouse – a gardener's "home away from home."

Double Decker Duplex (Don's, left); The Garden Shed (Kelly's, right)
Photos by Larry Merz

Jane Horton
Volunteer

One chilly autumn, searching for a soup recipe in an Italian cookbook, Jane, an accomplished cook and baker, was taken by all the beautiful homes and scenery shown next to the recipes. She had found her inspiration for a Tuscan habitat for the birds! Tireless in her many community activities, Jane, as well as contributing birdhouses, has also co-chaired the auction. A true, motivating force, she did an exemplary job, at the same time making it great fun for everyone involved.

per uccelli toscani

Photo by Anita Garnett

John BonSignore

Industrial Engineer, Educator

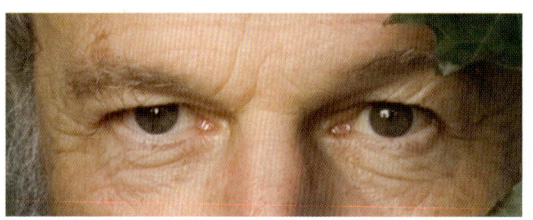

Each year, John constructs birdhouses using the simplest of materials and design, which are exquisitely sophisticated in execution, form and function. He uses wood, slate, stone and, sometimes, Plexiglass to make his delightful creations. John is an industrial designer and an internationally exhibited, award-winning sculptor, as well as a high school teacher.

Bon House V
Photos by Bruce Plotkin

Dawn Rogers
Doll Artist

Dawn Rogers brings her skills to bear with these two special works, Shamira and Lubomir. Shamira, guardian and protector, cares for a nest of fragile eggs representing the residents of Project Return, while Lubomir takes on the task of caring for and transporting his charges, and serves as a tribute to the volunteers and staff in helping the girls make their way forward in life. Such heartfelt inspiration is what makes the Birdhouse Auction such a special event for artists like Dawn.

Shamira: The Guardian and Protector

Lubomir (below)

Photos by Marcia Leverte

Wind (Walter's)
Uncle Sam (Naiad's)

Naiad & Walter Einsel

Artists, Illustrators

Naiad is world renowned as a graphic designer and illustrator whose work has been in magazines, books, TV commercials, commemorative stamps, games, and advertising. Her work has won 47 awards of Merit from the Society of Illustrators and has been extensively exhibited. She has taught at Parsons School of Design, Fairfield University and Silvermine School.

The late Walter Einsel was known widely as an illustrator, collagist and educator, although he also created wonderful pieces of sculpture in metal for the garden. He was particularly fond of composing art from found objects. He made kinetic sculptures of polished life-sized figures with moving parts– some with arms that reached around to offer an embrace!

Walter and Naiad were a perfect

87

Robert Goodenow
Retired Architect

Robert has created birdhouses every year for Project Return's auction and even though he now resides in Maryland, he still participates. His birdhouses are amazingly detailed and precise replicas of American icons– including an orange stand, a grist mill, and many local landmarks. He uses California redwood, specially-imported Spanish plywood (from Clementine boxes) and other materials, all carefully assembled.

Ye Yacht Yard (upper right)
McBird's (left)
The Robin's Grist Mill (left)
The Tanglewood Citrus Grove Birdhouse (left)
Bird Island Lighthouse (left)
Ogden House (left)
Hot Dog Heaven (right)
Victorian Cottage (left)

Photos by Mike Tewey

Eve Stockton

Architect, Printmaker, Sculptor

Eve is inspired by nature, science, myth and memory to create evocative paintings, prints and stone sculptures. Made of alabaster, soapstone and marble, her sculptures have sinuous shapes that suggest a latent energy and implied motion. Her paintings and prints are both about and of nature, evoked by the use of plant silhouettes and other natural forms. As for her birdhouses, Eve – also a trained architect – enjoys making them from what she calls the "crazy array of stuff" she finds in her studio.

The Augur-Water Bird (right)
Birdnesting (left)

Photos by Ted Horowitz

High school freshman, Tori Letzler, has been contributing to the Birdhouse Auction since she was in second grade. Her playful, imaginative birdhouse creations reflect her budding career in music and acting. It is natural that Tori, who will be touring in the United States in the 2006 Cirque de Soleil production "Quidam," chose a circus theme. Real circus tickets came with this circus birdhouse. Her birdhouses have often included special extras; some even turned the birdhouse, itself, into collectible memorabilia such as one adorned with autographs of stars from the Metropolitan Opera.

Chirpopolitan Opera (above)

Barnum & Birdie Circus (left); Hagrid's Hut (right)

Photos by Debra Somerville

Susan Malloy

Artist, Patron of the Arts

"I decided to make the 'Birdhouse Box' when a theme for a birdhouse didn't come to mind…also, I had this nice round box…" Susan creates art pieces and collages using wood and other materials. She focuses mainly on "clouds, water and trees, building up compositions that portray the mood of what she sees and feels." Susan has had nine important one-woman shows and has exhibited at the Hebrew Union College in New York City and at the Tang Museum of Art at Skidmore College.

The Birdhouse Box
Photo by Richard Frank

An artist, craft person and gardener, Susan said she began creating mosaics recently, and added a few shells to the pieces. After finding good sources of interesting shells, she began to focus on using shells instead of tile. She has been doing shell art for two years and finds it the most satisfying medium yet, "structured and spontaneous at the same time and in a very intimate scale." Her work has an elegance and richness of detail that makes it very special.

Royal Shell Pavilion

Photos by Pam Einarsen

Susan Lloyd
Crafter

Enid Munroe
Artist, Writer

Boutique d'Oiseaux (left page)
Ecole Des Oiseaux (left)
Domus Avium (below)

Photos by Alison Wachstein

Over the years, Enid's birdhouse creations have been described as chimerical, fabulous, imaginative, clever, inventive and sensational. She is a nationally known artist, gardener, lecturer and author of the book, *An Artist in the Garden*. Her work is included in such public collections as the National Museum of American Art in Washington, D.C., the Brooklyn Museum, The Hudson River School, the Hearst Corporation, Bank of America and Reader's Digest, among others.

Winston Potter

Artist, Publisher

Artist Winston Potter was inspired to create this delightful, heart- and hand-warming work by imagining the gentle act of kindness involved in tenderly picking up a wounded bird, in cupped hands. In publishing and art, he has given "work-minded people visual images." He received an award for his technical skill, imagination and radical departures in target chart presentation in World War II. He has had several shows of his sculpture, made mostly from found objects.

Bird-in-Hand

Photos by Debra K. Browne

Mike Tewey
Entrepreneur

A man-for-all-seasons: apparel business owner, consultant, sailor, accidental artist, photographer, Mike makes birdhouses for Project Return that reflect the variety of his skills. He has used all of his talents, working behind the scenes, to insure the continuing good work of Project Return.

Twister (this page & right)
Stone Garden

Photos by Bruce Ando

Artist Van Ruttley is a woodworker and artisan who owns a small furnishing and furniture business with a twist called Unique for You, in Darien. She takes "shabby chic" to a new level by turning antique items into pieces of furniture and accent pieces. Although Van works with materials of all kinds, she is especially proud of her birdhouse creations made from gourds raised by her own hand. "The idea of taking a piece of nature and transforming it into an object that could be used as a bowl, planter, basket or even as an art object, has become addictive."

Village 'Peep'-le

Photos by David Emberling

Van Ruttley
Artist, Woodworker

Ellen's artistic talents are focused on creating beautiful botanical collages using natural materials, pressed flowers and paper, combining them in arrangements to bring the outdoors in. She recently began creating jewelry to encase her miniature collages and discovered she loves the new medium! Her artwork is frequently found in fine art and craft shows.

Ellen Schiffman
Artist

Wee Precious House
Photos by Patrick Vingo

Kathi Sherman

Textile Artist

Kathi, an artist who works primarily in textile design, specializes in children's items. Her attention to detail and the funny slant she brings to her birdhouse subjects is captivating. "I enjoy creating satirical reproductions of Westport's interesting landmarks," says Kathy, who called her replica of the Westport Historical Society, the "Westport Hysterical Society." With the same good humor, Kathi, pictured here with "The Soggymuck Crowing Club," pokes fun at the Saugatuck Rowing Club. On closer inspection, one finds moving parts, and such items as a menu, guidebook and a 'twisted' version of the rowing anthem.

Soggymuck Crowing Club

Photos by Carol Verneuil

The County Store

Country Home

Boathouse II

Earl & Joey's Service Station

Dick Stein
Landscape Designer

Dick, landscape designer and contractor, makes birdhouses from old salvaged materials which resemble real historical buildings from America's past. The ideas for his birdhouses come from old books, magazines and photos. Once a house is completed, it is set outside for several months until it acquires the look of an antique. After the weathering process, the birdhouse is displayed indoors as further exposure could be detrimental. Dick has exhibited on Cape Cod and at the Annual Bird Carvers Festival.

Clay Toombs Bait & Tackle (near left)

Photos by Lorin Klaris

Robert Schwarz applied his talents in trompe d'oeil painting and woodworking to create this three dimensional birdhouse. "To me…the concept is more interesting than the actual finished project." It is easy to appreciate them both when you see this creation.

The Sketch

Photos by Peter Friedman

Robert Schwarz
Decorative Painter, Artist

"The birdhouses I have created are places where the spirit can be safe and at rest, places of nourishment for body and soul. In my work, I often use images of birds as symbols of the poetry and fragility of life. How nice to have had a chance to build a space to protect such treasures," says Ann. An exhibition of Ann's art "To Bear Witness" will be traveling to galleries and museums throughout the United States. She is represented by the Turner Carroll Gallery, Santa Fe, New Mexico, where she will be having a one person show.

Untitled (left), Return (right)

Photos by Pam Barkentin-Blackburn

Ann Weiner
Artist

The owner of Imagination Unlimited, Carol is an artist with an irreverent sense of humor, graphic design skills and the ability to encourage her young art students to let their creativity fly. With her students, she has built numerous miniatures, including circuses, cities, celtic elf communities, ancient civilizations and whole planets, complete with culture and energy systems. She often lets her own talents loose in shadow box libraries by commission. She created a special version of these boxes for Project Return entitled "Rara Avis Biblioteca."

Miggs B Birdhouse (above)
Rara Avis Bibliotheca

Photos by Kim Cooper

Carol Young

Artist, Educator

More Birdhouses…

A selection from the more than 2,000 birdhouses contributed to the auction over the last ten years.

Steve Lance, *Little Brown Bag* (photo by Alison Wachstein)

Gerianne Heinrich, *The Catbird Seat* (photo by Carol Verneuil)

Henry Goszkowski, *Tottenville Trolley* (photo by Alison Wachstein)

Judith Bacal, *Word House* (photo by Alison Wachstein)

Suzanne Ebeling-Urban, *Humpty Dumpty Sat on a Nest* (photo by Alison Wachstein)

Irene Henrick, *Bluebird at Dawn* (photo by Alison Wachstein)

Natasha Cohen, *Chopin's Dilemma* (photo by Miggs Burroughs)

Jon Westberg, *Jon's Ark (How high is the Water Mama?)* (photo by Alison Wachstein)

Judy Smith, *Comfort Food* (photo by Alison Wachstein)

Joan Denneen, *Home to Roost* (photo by Alison Wachstein)

Karen Brussat Butler, *Bird Villa* (photo by Alison Wachstein)

Carol Anthony, *Nest Box* (photo by Alison Wachstein)

Greg Puhy, *Totem Pole* (photo by Alison Wachstein)

Walt & Charlene Buttrick, *A Moment of Zen*
(photo by Alison Wachstein)

Elizabeth Burdick, *Flights of Fancy* (photo by Alison Wachstein)

Photographers

Bruce Ando (pages 54 & 102)
Ando Photography LLC
(203) 544-8954
www.andostock.com

Pam Barkentin-Blackburn (pages 20 & 114)
(203) 226-2857
www.pambo.net

Martha Bloom (page 64)
(203) 254-2020
e-mail: muvesz@aol.com

Debra K. Browne (pages 40 & 100)
(203) 834-0643
e-mail: rbrowne997@aol.com

Miggs Burroughs
(cover & pages 10, 18, 22, 34, 66, 119)
(203) 227-9667
www.miggsb.com
e-mail: miggsb@optonline.net

Kim Cooper (pages 28, 32, 86, 116)
(203) 247-4770
e-mail: kimcooper@aol.com

Pam Einarsen (page 46 & 96)
(203) 221-1818
www.pamelaeinarsen.com

David Emberling (pages 48 & 104)
David Emberling Studio
(203) 226-1836
www.davidemberling.net
e-mail: davidemberling@optonline.net

Robin Fellows (page 16)
Photojournalist
(203) 221-8489
e-mail: rfellows7@optonline.net

Andrea Maritzer Fine (page 26)
(203) 454-7760
www.absolutearts.com/andreafine
email: andreafine@optonline.net

Richard Frank (page 94)
(203) 227-0496
e-mail: Richard@richardfrank.com

Peter Friedman (pages 42 & 112)
Peter Friedman Photographer
(203) 227-4595

Anita Garnett (page 80)
Anita Garnett Photography
(860) 379-4145
www.anitagarnett.com

Mary Ellen Hendricks (page 38)
(203) 259-5507
www.maryellenhendricks.com
e-mail: maryellenhendricks@yahoo.com

Ron Henkin (page 36)
Images In Photography
(203) 255-2602
www.Homepage.mac.com/RonHenkin

John Hill (page 44)
John F. Hill Fine Photography
(203) 545-6069
25 Old Stonewall Rd, Easton, Ct. 06612
e-mail: John @johnfhill.com

Ted Horowitz (page 90)
Ted Horowitz Photography
(203) 454-8766,
e-mail: ted@horowitzphoto.com

Roger Spencer Jones (page 62)
(203) 520-4771
e-mail: send2photographer@hotmail.com

David Kalman (pages 30 & 50)
Fine Art Photographer, (203) 227-7731
www.PhotographybydKalman.com
e-mail: dkalman@optonline.net

Lorin Klaris (pages 12, 14 & 110)
Lorin Klaris Photography
7 Ludlow Road, Westport, CT 06880
(203) 227-9683
e-mail: lklaris@optonline.net

Marcia Leverte (page 84)
"FACES" Photography by Marcia
(203) 221-7608

Larry Merz (pages 56 & 78)
(203) 222-1936
www.larrymerzphoto.com

Morgaine Pauker (page 70)
(203) 454-9559
e-mail: morgainep@optonline.net

Bruce Plotkin (pages 60 & 82)
Bruce Plotkin Photography
(203) 454-1143
www.bruceplotkin.com,
e-mail: bruce@bruceplotkin.com

Debra Somerville (pages 76 & 92)
Debra Somerville Photography
203) 226-5961
www.debrasomerville.com
e-mail: photo4kdz@aol.com

Mike Tewey (cover & pages 52, 72, 74, & 88)
(see artist page 102)

Carol Verneuil (pages 68, 108 & 118)
(203) 226-3455
e-mail: jvernevi@optonline.net

Patrick Vingo (pages 24 & 106)
Patrick Vingo: Photographs
(203) 866-3895

Alison Wachstein
(cover & pages 98 & 118-121)
(203) 226-5296
e-mail: alison@alisonwachstein.com

Hans Wilhelm (page 58)
(see artist page 18)

Creators & Contributors of Birdhouse Auction Items

A.C. Moore
Lucy Ackemann
Acqua Restaurant
Chip Adams
Carol Adornetto
Jack Adornetto
Sandra Agate
Agents of William Raveis Real Estate
Troy Aikman
Marian Ainsworth
Frederick Albee III
Robert Aldrich
Charlotte Allen
Thelma Allen
Diana Anastasopoulos
Amy Ancel
Joni Andrews
Debbi Angotti
Carol Anthony
Anthropologie
Architectural Digest
Lisa Arnold
Ron Arnold
Deborah Atkins
Atlantic National Mortgage Company
Nancy Austin
Valerie Austyn
Curtiss Avery
Janet Heim Avery
Stephanie Babcock
Amy Babkie
Judith Bacal
Betsy Back
Carolyn Baker
Marshall Baldwin
Barbara Bangser
Susan Baron
Blair Barone
Courtney Barone
Mary Ann Barr
Lynn Barrie
Zara Barrie
Roger Bartels

Susie Basler
Frank Basler
Mary Bauman
Joan Beauvais
Janice Beavers
Tomi Beck
Bedford Builders Club
Bedford Middle School Students
Liz Beeby
Alison Beispel
Kate Beispel
Harry Belafonte
Judie Bell
Sharon Bell
Deena Bellman
Geoff Bellman
Matt Benson
Rick Benson
R.B. Benson
Totney Benson
Nina Bentley
Richard Bentley
Don Bergman
Susan Berkowitz
Carol Berkowitz
Linda Scinto
Elaine Best
Gloria Biagiotti
Aldo Biagiotti
Richard Biliack
Birdnest of Ridgefield
Binnie Birstein
Jody Bishel
Elise Black
Lisa Black
Karen Silver Bloom
Martha Bloom
Blue Fish
Linda Blum
Bobbie-que Restaurant
Michael Bolton
John BonSignore
Christie Lynn Botti
Victoria Botti
Mary Bouscaren

Ted Bowman
Brandman's Paint & Decorating
Dominique Brazier
Joseph Breisler
Laura Brengelman
John Brengelman
Carol Brezovec
Jennifer Brezovec
Julia Broder
Meg Brogdan
Ron Brogden
Gail Brookover
Marsha Brooker
Bonnie Brooks
Mona Brown
Sallie Hackett Brown
Chance Browne

Joanne & Paul. Photo by Miggs Burroughs

Debra Browne
Linda Bruce
Frank Bruckman
Karen Brussat-Butler
Morgan Bryant
Linda Bryk
Bungalow
Elizabeth Burdick
Arthur Burke
Geraldine Burke
Leslie Burke
Ryan Burke
Miggs Burroughs
Sue Buruchian
Andrea Busk
Fred Busk
Barbara Butler
Charlene Buttrick

Walt Buttrick
Andrea Byrne
Tony Cadman
John Caggiano
Linda Cahan
Denise Callahan
Carol Caputo
Rich Cardinal
Trina Parker Cardinal
Jane Carlin
Emily Carpenter
Sharon Carpenter
Barbara Carr
Jamison Cash
Nancy Cash
Lorraine Casscles
Linn Cassetta
Cast of "60 Minutes II"
Cast of "The View"
Castle Wine & Spirits
Center for Healing & Recovery
Melissa Cetlin
Diana Chamberlain
Maryann Charmoz
Remy Charmoz
Jade Hobson Charnin
Kathy Charron
Jillian Cheney
Ann Chernow
Jim Cherry
John Choly
Sharon Christie
Charlotte Frazen Ciaraldi
Jay Cimbak
Angela Ciriello
Cindy Citrone
Jan Clark
Isabella Clavelous
Serge Clement
Barbara Cmiel
Carol Cohen
Lewis Cohen
Marilyn Cohen
Natasha Cohen
Carla Cohn

Coleman & Kohn Antiques
Coleytown Middle School 7th Grade (1997)
Kylie Collins
Kim Cooper
Pam Cooper
Coreen's Bridge Floral
Pat Costanzo
Helene Cote
Pat Coulson
Country Living Magazine
Alyssa Crouse
Laurie Crouse
Martin Crouse
Thomas Cummings
Raynor Cunningham
Curio Cottage, Westport Women's Club
Kathy Curioli
Paul Curioli
Adele Cutrali-Valovich
Emily D'Alessio
Robert Dancik
Lisa Daugherty
Paige Davison
Daybreak Nurseries, Ltd.
Jose DeAndrade
Annie DeKraker
Michele Del Grande
Steve Delay
Linda Dempsey
Jean Denholz
Joan Denneen
Derma Clinic
Paul Desmardis
Jennifer Desmond
Susan Desmond
Devonshire
Cathy DiDonato
Morgan DiDonato
Michelle Dinan
Sara Dinkin
Domain
Meredith Donaher
Linda Donaldson

Pauline Downing
Ted Downing
Sean Doyle
Stan Drake
Marion Drexler
Milton Drexler
Tish Duffy
Laura Dufour
John Dumke
Joan Dushinske
Helene Dworski
Kelly Dwyer
EarthAnimal
Earthplace
Suzanne Ebeling-Urban
Susana Echeverria-Corlett
Joanna Ecke
Julia Eckman
Barbara Eden
Karen Eichoff
Roger Eichoff
Naiad Einsel
Walter Einsel
Jean-Peirre Eischan
Annalee Emanuel
Herzl Emanuel
Caitlin Emro
Rosemarie Emro
Roy Erhardt
Elmer Eriksson
Jeanine Esposito
Jean Everett
John Everett
Wendy Cook Everett
Pat Everson
Everything Personalized
Jim Ezzes
Ann Faber
Catherine Fabryk
Kathy Fagella
Vin Fagella
Andrew Fahrland
Katherine Fairbanks
Fairfield Boy Scout Troop #90
Family Album
Diane Farrell
Jose Feliciano & Family

Maynard Ferguson
Manny Ferriera
Jody Fidler
Carolyn Field
Jocelyn Fifield
John Fifield
Joe Fili
Bill Finch
Andrea Fine
Betsy Finley
Thomas Finley
Hugh Fiorato
Katherine Fischer
Marti Fischer
Ben Fisher
Jan Fisher
Kenneth Fisher
Sam Fisher
Henry Fisher
Marta Flavin
Mr. Fleischer
Richard Flowers
David Flynn
Food For Thought
Richard Foot
Karen Ford
Kassie Foss
Larry Foss
Eileen Carnes Foster
Corey Fountain
Fovama Rugs
Dick Frank
Leona Frank
Deborah Fratino
Fred Fricke
Mary Fricke
Howard Friedman
Marianne Frisch
Richard Frisch
Juliana Fulbright
Mary Beth Fyda
Faith Gaertner
Don Gans
Jan Gans
Rick Garcia
Garden Center of Darien
Carol Garey

Ira Garey
Josh Garey
Kent Garland
Brie Garrison
Haley Garrison
Morgan Garrison
Harriett Gartner
Gene Gavin
Melissa Gelman
Stephanie Gelman-Lippert
Tancy Gemsa
Dorinda Germade
Dylan Germade
Sinclaire Germade
Karen Gersch
Gilbertie's Herb Garden
Gail Gilcrest
Linda Gilleran

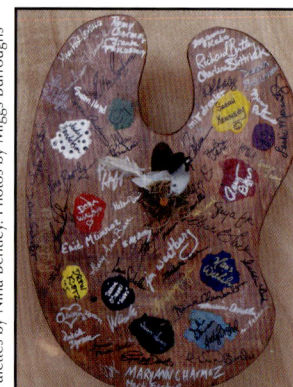
Palettes by Nina Bentley. Photos by Miggs Burroughs

Aurele Gilleran
Judy Gilmartin-Willsey
Girl Scout Troop #313
Girl Scout Troop #369
Leslie Giuliani
Marianne Gjersvick
Abbye Goldberg
Steve Goldberg
Terry Lewis Goldberg
Good Dimension
Robert Goodenow
Shirlee Gordon
Henry Goszkowski
Bruce Graham
Ellen Granger
Liz Granger
Tom Granger

Midge Grant
Al Gratrix
Al Gratrix Sr.
Barbara Gray
Edward Gray
John Grdinich
Nicole Grdinich
Annabell Green
Greens Farms Liquor
Greg & Tony Salon
H & B Birdbarns
Hope Hageman
Dorita Hahnfeldt
Connie Haines
Inglis Eman Hale
Roe Halper
Clark Hanford
Greg Hauton
Tammy Hawkins
Holly Hawthorn
Jackie Hayes
Margot Hayward
Madeline Hazelwood
HB Home
Julie Hedge
Karen Heffner
Thea Heilbron
Valerie Heilbron
Gerianne Heinrich
Heirloom Designs
Paul Held
Susan Hendee
Jennifer Henderson
Judy Henderson
Shaun Henderson
Sarah Henderson
Gail Hennessy
Irene Henrick
Suzanne Henrick
Debora Herdic
Barbara (Bobbie) Herman
Scott Herman
Greta Hentsch-Cowles
Kim Heyl
Paul Hicks
Barry Himmel
Jared Himmel

Julie Himmel
Marc Himmel
Don Hodges
Dustin Hoffman
Ann Holmes
Homebuilder's Association
Richard Hooke
Janet Horowitz
Leonard Horowitz
Jane Horton
Martin Howard
Ann Howden
Joyce Howell
Lance Huber (Braeland)
Julie Huber
Chuck Huddleston
Stacey Hughes
Susan Hulls
Betsy Hulme
Tasha Hutchinson
Priscilla Igram
Quinn Igram
Virginia Irwin
Joe Italiano
Kristen Jaeckle
Judy James
Julianne Jenkins
Derek Jeter
Mimi John
Noah Johnson
Judy Juracek
Marcie Juran
Brian Kabcenell
Suzanne Kahn
Dick Kalaman
David Kalman
Marina Kamina
Jennifer Kanter
Sandy Kapell
Jim Kardas
Natasha Karpinskaia
Alice Katz
Judith Katz
Barry Katz
Robin Katzman
Arnie Kaye
Grace Kehle

Michael Keith
Sarah Keller
Dan Keller
Doreen Kelly
John Kelly
Sheila Kelly
Mariann Kennedy
Sarah Kennedy
Elise Khatchian
Constance Kiermaier
Faye Kim
Kismet
Roger Kizik
Lorin Klaris
Susan Klau
Lucy Klinga
Ed Klinga
Audrey Klotz
Drew Klotz
Dan Klyver
Koenig Alexandra
Lorraine Kohanowich
Alexander Kohanowich
Adam Konowitz
Noel Konrad
Mary Korotash
Roy Kortick
Senja Kosci
Ed Koucco
Jak Kovatch
Randy Kraft
Meg Krakowiak
Sally Kranz
Andrew Kromelow
Lucy Krupenye
Joseph Krygier
Abbey Lake
Kelly Lamb
Susan Lamy
Dan Lance
Steve Lance
Shar Landers
John LaPick
Ann Lathrop
Carter Lathrop
Howard Lathrop
Niles Lathrop

Deb Laurino
John Laurino
Betsy Laurino
Jennifer Laurino
Susan Laventhal
Paola Lazzaro
Cate Leach
Bill Leach
Joanne Leaman
Diane Lederer
Isabelle Lee
Alison Lerch
Tori Letzler
Marcia Letzler
Maureen Lewis
Betsy Lewittes
Lillian August
Jerry Liotta
Robin Liotta
Susan Lloyd
Karen Loprete
Mary Rose Lovello
Connie Lowenstein
John Loynes
Bill Lucas
Helen Luedke
John Luscombe
Ed Lynn
Maryanne Magner
Susan Malloy
David Manente
Jilda Manikas
Elizabeth Mann
Kathy Maple
Leslie Marantz
Geraldine Marcenyac
Carole Marchese
Linda Martin
Richard Mastropietro
George Masumian
Jaqueline Masumian
Andrea Mathewson
Jeff Mayer & Family
Henry Mayo
Doba Mazo
Diane McCallister
Chris McCarthy

Anne McCutcheon
Margaret McKinnickkinnick
Mary McLaughlin
Ellen McNeely
Kathleen McNichols-Marks
Sandra Meagher
Josephine Meckseper
Kathleen Mermy
Rene Metcalf
Laura Meyer
Paula Meyer
Wally Meyer
Elizabeth Meyer
Gordon Micunis
David Miles
Joan Miller
Marcia Miller
Audrey Miller

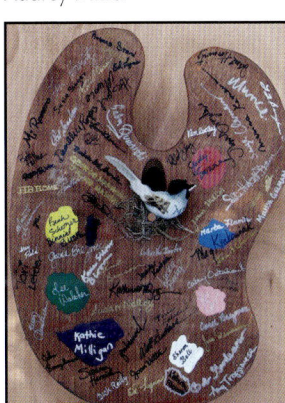

Kathie Milligan
Suzanne Mikulka
Mimi Designs
Mitchell's of Westport
Dominick Modugno
Lise Molinari
Melanie Montgomery
Mary Tyler Moore
Gus Moran
Julie Mori
Jean Mortensen
Joyce Mueller
Ted Mueller
Andrew Munce
Howard Munce
Enid Munroe
Chris Murphy

Laura Murphy
Catherine Murray
Matt Murray
George Muscolino
Gene Musicus
Bonnie Musicus
Tom Nadeau
Diane Nash
Julie Naughton
Cris Negrin
Betsy Neuburg
Lissy Newman
Paul Newman
Debra Newsom
Peggy Newsham
Nga Nguyen
Nancy Noonan
Jeanne Norell
Not Just Pink
Rea Nurmi
Denise O'Connell
Pat O'Malley
Kacey O'Reilly
Mary O"Reilly
Carrie Ann Oldani
Cornelia Olsen
Cathy Osterhout
Phillipe Otello
Karen Outerson
Mark Owades
Samantha Owades
Barbara Owen
Hossein Paktinat
Arnold Palmer
Peter Palmer
Eileen Panepinto
Richard Paris
Kathy Parker
Robert Parker
Marie Partington
Alison Patrick
Manny Pattavina
Rose Pattavina
Fiorenza Paul
Lynn H. Peer
David Perman
Flo Perry

Stephanie Peterson
Jennifer Petrosinelli
Michele Petruno
Regis Philbin
Lily Philpot
Pickets
Ted Piker
Dorota Pilchowska
Amy Pines
Greg Pollack
Jane Pollack
Terry Porter
Frank Posluszny
Winston Potter
Martha Potts
Pound Ridge Nursery
Carmen Prelee
Suzanne Propp
Psychoanalysis Institute
Alexandra Puchala
Greg Puhy
Purple Feet
Robert Quackenbush
Don Quatrella
Kelly Quatrella
Saba Quraishi
Libby Rackcliff
Pat Rackliffe
Harry Rappaport
William Raveis
Catherine Raymond
Realtors of Prudential
    Real Estate
Diane Reddin
Marilee Reilly
Dick Reilly
Christine Reinholz
Martha Reinken
Catherine Sylvia Reiss
Residents and Staff of
    Project Return
Marilyn Rice-Lister
Ridgefield Center for Families
    & Children
Amy Riggio
Carolyn Roberti
Suzanne Roberts

Timothy Robinson
Lark Elizabeth Rodriques
Dawn Alice Rogers
Kenny Rogers
Tina Rohrer
Margaret Roleke
Fantasia Romano
Gerald Romano
Cathy Romano
Mi Romero
Nancy Rosaldo
Charlie Rose
Audrey Rosenberg
Andrew Rosenblatt
Katherine Ross
Sheila Ross
Bill Rowe
Tony Rubin
Chiara Rudzin
John Russo
Linda Russo
Van Ruttley
Catherine Ryan
Tom Sacks
Lucy Sallick
Anne Salthouse
Barbara Sands
Saugatuck Rowing Club
Ken Savage
Joseph Saviano
Patricia Scanlan
Debra Schaffer
Lewis Schaffer
Bill Scheffler
Leah Scherzer
Ellen Schiffman
Rebecca Schneider
Richard Schneider
Philip Schockley
Joelle Schon
Gabriella Schulman
Rin Schwartz
Robert Schwarz
Carol Schweid
Wayne Scott
Leslie Sears
Carol Seha

Lynn Sellon
Jaclyn Sharp
Matt Shean
Ann Sheffer
Susan Sheinbaum
Shelton Brownie Troop #1084
Shelton Girl Scout Troop #830
Shelton Girl Scout Troop #860
David Sher
Nancy Sherian
Guy Sherman
Kathi Sherman
John Shuck
Susan Siegel
Dolores Siegel
Jody Silver
Silver's of Westport
Susan Simms
JoAnn Simon
Simply Country
Sue Singer
Diane Sjoblom
Lee Skalkos-Baldyga
Drew Skarupa
Ty Skarupa
Geri Skinner
John Skinner
Vicky Sloat
Louis Slovinski
Rita Smircich
Judy Smith
Patricia Smith
Peggy Smith
Ann Smith-Goodwin
Joan Snyder
Reene Cr Soni
B.J. Sottes
Ellin Spadone
Elaine Hay Spicer
Robin Spielberg
Susan Spivack
David Squires
Susan St. James
John Staheli
Consuelo Staneli
John Staneli
Richard Staneski

Kathy Stanski
Dick Stein
Maryanne Stell
Nancy Stember
Peter Stephens
Jim Steuerlein
Katie Stevenson
Stew Leonard's
Nancy Stewart
Martha Stewart
Michael Stickley
Eve Stockton
Debi Stockwell
Andrea Stone
Courtney Storty
Ann Stratton
Kassia Strauss
Florence Suerig
Billie Jean Sullivan

Tori Letzler. Photo by Debra Somerville

Meg Sullivan
Susan's Cookie Shop
Judy Swann
Talking Heads
Tarantino's Restaurant
Kim Tarnapoll
John Taylor
Jeannette Tewey
Mike Tewey
The Evergreen Shop
The Ivy Urn
The World's Smallest
    Ad Agency
Robert Thomas
Jeannie Thomma
Cheryl Tiegs
Philip Topalian
Town Nails

Amy Traggianese
Bud Trenka
Amber Treschitta
Jody Treschitta
John Treschitta
Mary Treschitta
Harriett Troesser
Karla Troesser
Jon Troesser
Frank Trzaskos
Yoka Trzaskos
Janice Tuckman
Maureen Tumminello
Vincent Tumminello
U.S. Surgical
Julie Uman
Jonathan Uman
Suzanne Underwood
Dina Upton
Mike Urban
Baxter Urist
Sara Usilton
Pat Van de Graff
Annie Van der Ven
Heather Van Deusen
Mimi Van Deusen
Christina Van Duijn
Lucas Van Zanten
Nora Lee Vayser
Luis Velez
Verde
Tom Veronesi
Jerry Vigorito
Laurie Vogel
Jeff Von Kohorn
Joan Votta
Alison Wachstein
Liz Wachstein
Cheryl Wade
William Wainright
Jodi Wallace
Dora Walsh
Martha Link Walsh
Lee Walther
Lorraine Ward-Copley
John Waski
Gar Waterman

Waterworks
Cheryl Watson
Monica Wayne
Ann Weiner
Robert Weinmann
Caleb Weiss
Zack Weiss
Gloria Weld
Jon Westberg
Weston Elementary School,
    Ms. Casey's 3rd Grade
    Class, 2002
Weston Girl Scout Troop #194
Weston Girl Scout Troop #194
Weston Junior Girl Scout
    Troop #640
Dirk Westphal
Westport Brownie Troop #48
Westport Girl Scout Troop #548
Westport Girl Scout Troop #659
Westport Marketing
Westport Weston YMCA
Joan Wheeler
Rosemary Whidden
Gene Wilder
Roger Wilder
Vickie Wilder
Hans Wilhelm
Barbara Wilk
Mark Wilkerson
Woody Wilkins
Bobbie Williams
Robin Williams
Tinea Williams
Carolyn Wilson
Joanne Woodward
Woodworkers Club of Norwalk
Marjorie Yeaple
Gretchen Yengst
Carol Young
Elizabeth Youngling
Roberta Zelikow
Ryan Zygmont

Owners of the Featured Birdhouses

Rick Benson
Bye Bye Birdie – From the collection of Ann Sheffer and Bill Scheffler
A Victorian Home – From the collection of Betsy and Watts Wacker
Waldheim Camp (Adirondack House) — From the collection of Ann Sheffer and Bill Scheffler
Saugatuck Harbor Yacht Club – From the collection of Patricia and Jeffrey Scanlan

Nina & Richard Bentley
Birdie Hole – From a private collection
Building Plans Approved: The Planning & Dozing Committee – From the collection of Judy & Larry Prince
Stool Pigeon – From the collection of Patty Burrows and Milton Wolfson
Location, Location, Location — From the collection of Bonnie & Jim Whittemore
Louis Tweet-ton — From the collection of Teresa Lin and Craig Knight
Welcome to Wallport – From the collection of Al and Hope Hageman

Elise Black
Elements — From the collection of Patty Burrows and Milton Wolfson

Karen Silver Bloom
Temptation — From the collection of Rick and Totney Benson
And They Lived Happily Ever After — From the collection of Rick and Totney Benson
Childlife — From the collection of Noel and Bruce Konrad

Martha Bloom
Untitled – From the collection of Carol Young

John BonSignore
Bon House V — From the collection of Rod and Judy Smith

Carol Brezovec & Cathy Osterhout
Birdhouse Topiary — From the collection of Ann Sheffer and Bill Scheffler
Funky Feathers – From the collection of Nancy Austin
Fancy Feathers – From the collection of Ann Sheffer and Bill Scheffler

Sallie Hackett Brown
Das Blau Bird Bauhaus — From the collection of Kim Cooper and Mark Owades

Arthur Burke
Faberge Aviary – From a private collection
Singer's Aviary – From the collection of Rick and Totney Benson
Cornell House for Birds — From the collection of Patty Burrows and Milton Wolfson

Miggs Burroughs
Unopened Rose — From the collection of Patricia and Jeffrey Scanlan
Changes – From the collection of Kim Cooper and Mark Owades
Tender Treasures — From the collection of Maureen and Jeff Cook
The Gift — From the collection of Patricia and Jeffrey Scanlan

Maryann Charmoz
The Gourdy Bird Family – From a private collection

Ann Chernow
Designer Hen – From the collection of Sue Galati

Lewis & Marilyn Cohen
De Oily Boid – From the collection of Diane and Kevin Connolly
Bird Watcher – From the collection of Deena and Jeff Bellman
Art is for the Birds – From a private collection
The White-Crested, Migratory, Sun-Seeking Snowbird – From the collection of Renee Gold

Steve Delay
Birds Eye Birdhouse — From the collection of Patty Burrows and Milton Wolfson

Meredith Donaher
Seaside Cottage — From the collection of Judy and George Sterling

Helene Dworski
Bead Bird – From the collection of Teresa Lin and Craig Knight
Wing Chair – From a private collection

Naiad & Walter Einsel
Uncle Sam — From the collection of James Ezzes
Wind — From the collection of Ann Sheffer and Bill Scheffler

Marta Flavin
Compo Beach & Classic Home – From the collection of Jen and Jon Nicolazzo

Richard Flowers
Rustic Retreat – From a private collection

Kassie & Larry Foss
Cape Cod Contentment — From the collection of Mike & Jeannette Tewey
Old Town Hall — From the collection of James Ezzes
English Style Stone Cottage – From the collection of Renee Gold

Leslie Giuliani
Bird Sanctuary — From the collection of Miggs Burroughs

Robert Goodenow
Ye Yacht Yard — From a private collection
McBird's — From the collection of Rick and Totney Benson
The Robin's Grist Mill — From the collection of Patty Burrows and Milton Wolfson
The Tanglewood Citrus Grove Birdhouse — From the collection of Patty Burrows and Milton Wolfson

Bird Island Lighthouse — From a private collection
Ogden House — From a private collection
Hot Dog Heaven — From a private collection
Victorian Cottage — From a private collection

Judy Henderson & Hans Wilhelm
Freedom Bird – From the private collection of Deena & Jeff Bellman
The Moon & Other Fantasies – From the collection of Mike & Jeannette Tewey
Matilda — From the collection of Mike & Jeannette Tewey
Papagena (white ceramic) — From the collection of Mike & Jeannette Tewey
Jack's Birdhouse – From a private collection

Suzanne Henrick
Spring Rain Storm—Seeking Shelter — From the collection of Renee Gold

Barbara (Bobbie) Herman
Stars & Stripes – From the collection of Melissa Gelman

Jane Horton
per uccelli toscani — From the collection of Diane and Kevin Connolly

Constance Kiermaier
Fly Away Home — From the collection of Rick and Totney Benson
Forest Birdhouse – From the collection of Richard & Nina Bentley

Drew & Audrey Klotz
Fried Chicken — From the collection of Kim Cooper and Mark Owades
Moulin Rouge — From the collection of Kim Cooper and Mark Owades

Lucy Krupenye
Zen Shelter II – From the collection of Jeanine Esposito and Frederic Chiu

Tori Letzler

Barnum & Birdie Circus — From a private collection

Chirpopolitan Opera — From the collection of Pearl & Henry Owades

Hagrid's Hut — From the collection of Teresa Lin and Craig Knight

Susan Lloyd

Royal Shell Pavilion — From the collection of Suzanne Henrick

Susan Malloy

The Birdhouse Box — From the collection of Mimi Van Deusen

Howard & Andrew Munce

The Stool Pigeon House — From the collection of Patty Burrows and Milton Wolfson

The Bird-Brain House — From the collection of Kim Cooper and Mark Owades

Enid Munroe

Domus Avium — From the collection of Ann Sheffer and Bill Scheffler

Ecole Des Oiseaux — From the collection of Kim Cooper and Mark Owades

Boutique d'Oiseaux — From the collection of Joe and Maggie Feczko

Paul Newman & Joanne Woodward

A Home is for Family — From the collection of Eva and Paul Rosenblatt

A Home for All — From the collection of Teresa Lin and Craig Knight

Manny Pattavina

The Sanctuary — From the collection of Mike & Jeannette Tewey

Winston Potter

Bird-in-Hand — From the collection of Rick and Totney Benson

Kelly & Don Quatrella

Double Decker Duplex — From the collection of Don and Jane Horton

The Garden Shed — From the collection of Olivia and Wes Dunn

Dick Reilly

The Crofter's Cottage — From the collection of Teresa Lin and Craig Knight

Bound for Glory — From a private collection

Bronson Windmill — From the collection of Bob and Brie Garrison

Call Box 911 — From the collection of Eve & Ed Reilly

Amy Riggio

Time Flies II — From the collection of Joan Votta

Dawn Alice Rogers

Shamira: The Guardian and Protector — From the collection of Patty Burrows and Milton Wolfson

Lubomir — From the collection of Marcia and Bob Leverte

Katherine Ross

Nina's Wings — From the collection of Joe and Maggie Feczko

Woven — From a private collection

Van Ruttley

Village 'Peep'-le — From the collection of Jeff and Karen Butler

Lucy Sallick

Charming the Birds — From the collection of Patricia and Jeffrey Scanlan

Secret Designs — From the collection of Susie and Frank Basler

Our House — From the collection of Susie and Frank Basler

Patricia Scanlan

Tweet Tweet Bling Bling — From the collection of Sue and Ed Reilly

Compo Pavilion — From the collection of Roe Colletti

Luminest — From the collection of Patty Burrows and Milton Wolfson

The Iris Cottage — From a private collection

Ellen Schiffman

Wee Precious House — From a private collection

Robert Schwarz

The Sketch — From the collection of Deena and Jeff Bellman

Kathi Sherman

Soggymuck Crowing Club — From the collection of Winslow & Diane Farrell

Dick Stein

The County Store — From a private collection

Boathouse II — From a private collection

Country Home — From the collection of Maureen and Jeff Cook

Clay Toombs Bait & Tackle — From the collection of Rick and Totney Benson

Earl & Joey's Service Station — From a private collection

Eve Stockton

The Augur-Water Bird — From the collection of The Anderson Family

Birdnesting — From the collection of Rick and Totney Benson

Michael Tewey

Twister — From the collection of Jeff and Karen Butler

Stone Garden — From the collection of Patricia and Jeffrey Scanlan

John Waski

Scream – From a private collection

Cat House – From a private collection

Ann Weiner

Return (with small doll) — From the collection of Patty Burrows and Milton Wolfson

Untitled — From the collection of Patty Burrows and Milton Wolfson

Carol Young

Rara Avis Bibliotheca — From the collection of Joe and Maggie Feczko

Miggs B Birdhouse — From the collection of Miggs Burroughs

More Birdhouses

Carol Anthony

Nest Box — From the collection of Patricia and Jeffrey Scanlan

Judith Bacal

Word House — From the collection of Maggie and Joe Feczko

Elizabeth Burdick

Flights of Fancy — From the collection of Teresa Lin and Craig Knight

Karen Brussat Butler

Bird Villa — From the collection of Carol and David Fishman

Walt & Charlene Buttrick

A Moment of Zen — From the collection of Carol Brezovec

Natasha Cohen

Chopin's Dilemma — From the collection of Nina and Richard Bentley

Joan Denneen

Home to Roost — From the collection of Judy Zwieback

Suzanne Ebeling-Urban

Humpty Dumpty Sat on a Nest — From the collection of Jeannette and Michael Tewey

Henry Goszkowski

Tottenville Trolley — From the collection of Rick and Totney Benson

Gerianne Heinrich

The Catbird Seat — From the collection of Deb & John Laurino

Irene Henrick

Bluebird at Dawn — From the collection of Eva and Paul Rosenblatt

Steve Lance

Little Brown Bag — From the collection of Eva and Paul Rosenblatt

Greg Puhy

Totem Pole — From the collection of Hope and Al Hageman

Judy Smith

Comfort Food — From the collection of Patty Burrows and Milt Wolfson

Jon Westberg

Jon's Ark (How high is the Water Mama?) — From the collection of Patricia and Jeffrey Scanlan